Dear Parent:
Your child's love of reading starts here!

Every child learns to read in a different way and at his or her own speed. Some go back and forth between reading levels and read favorite books again and again. Others read through each level in order. You can help your young reader improve and become more confident by encouraging his or her own interests and abilities. From books your child reads with you to the first books he or she reads alone, there are I Can Read Books for every stage of reading:

SHARED READING
Basic language, word repetition, and whimsical illustrations, ideal for sharing with your emergent reader

BEGINNING READING
Short sentences, familiar words, and simple concepts for children eager to read on their own

READING WITH HELP
Engaging stories, longer sentences, and language play for developing readers

READING ALONE
Complex plots, challenging vocabulary, and high-interest topics for the independent reader

ADVANCED READING
Short paragraphs, chapters, and exciting themes for the perfect bridge to chapter books

I Can Read Books have introduced children to the joy of reading since 1957. Featuring award-winning authors and illustrators and a fabulous cast of beloved characters, I Can Read Books set the standard for beginning readers.

A lifetime of discovery begins with the magical words **"I Can Read!"**

Visit www.icanread.com for information
on enriching your child's reading experience.

To parents who will be reading
this book to your children—
RAP IT!

I'm Rappy the Raptor
and I'd like to say,
I may not talk
in the usual way.

RAPPY

Goes to the Library

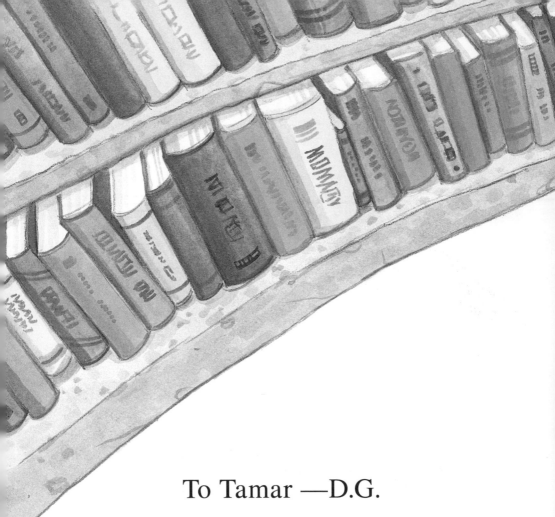

To Tamar —D.G.

To my good friend Amy Deeds —T.B.

I Can Read Book® is a trademark of HarperCollins Publishers.

Rappy Goes to the Library
Text copyright © 2017 by Dan Gutman
Illustrations copyright © 2017 by Tim Bowers
All rights reserved. Manufactured in China.
No part of this book may be used or reproduced in any manner whatsoever without written permission except in the case of
brief quotations embodied in critical articles and reviews. For information address HarperCollins Children's Books, a division of
HarperCollins Publishers, 195 Broadway, New York, NY 10007.
www.icanread.com

ISBN 978-0-06-225266-1 (hardcover)—ISBN 978-0-06-225265-4 (pbk.)

17 18 19 20 21 SCP 10 9 8 7 6 5 4 3 2 1   ❖   First Edition

HarperCollins
PUBLISHERS
Since 1817

RAPPY

Goes to the Library

by Dan Gutman

illustrated by Tim Bowers

HARPER

An Imprint of HarperCollinsPublishers

I'm rapping on vacation.

I'm rapping at home.

I'm rapping in Paris.

I'm rapping in Rome.

Mrs. Hooperlooper is my teacher
(a huge and terrifying creature).
She said, "Put away your notes.
And everybody, get your coats!"

"Grab your lunch and snacks,"
she cried.

"Today we're going for a ride!"

We drove and drove a million hours,

in the sun and in rain showers.

We rode a train and flew a jet.

I shouted out, "Are we there yet?"

I'll tell you, it was one long trip.

We even took a rocket ship!

Okay, all of that didn't happen.

I got caught up in my rappin'!

There was no train or jet or ferry.

We just went to . . .

. . . the library!

Mrs. H. said, "Shhhhh! Be quiet!
You don't want to start a riot.
Everyone should make good choices.
Only use your inside voices."

"My name is Mrs. Darien,"
said a very nice librarian.
Mrs. D. said, "Glad to meet you"
and "I promise not to eat you."

"Welcome to the library!

The best part is, the books are free!

You don't have to pay a dime.

Just take the books.

It's not a crime."

Checking books out isn't hard
once you have this little card.
We all had to wait in line.
Mrs. D. then gave me mine.
I was oh so very happy.
On the front my card said "Rappy."

So many books are on the shelf!

I can't count them all myself.

"Do you have books on foreign lands?"

"Yes, but kids should raise their hands."

"Is there a book about a cow?"

"Yes, but we're not reading now."

"Boats? Planes? Volcanoes erupting?"

"Will you please stop interrupting?"

I was getting nasty looks

when I asked about the books.

Mrs. D. gave us a tour.

We had to look at every floor.

I wasn't gonna make a peep.

But half the class was half asleep!

Everything was such a bore!

I think I heard a few kids snore.

Mrs. D. was nearly weeping

when she noticed kids were sleeping.

When I saw the kids all napping,

I decided to start rapping. . . .

Take a look at all these books!

Books that are fiction!

Books that are fact!

Books that help you to relax!

Some are silly!

Some are scary!

Some have little houses

on the prairie!

There are books about knitting!

And books about sewing!

And books about anything

that's worth knowing!

Stories are set
in all kinds of places.
Like under the sea
and in outer spaces!

Some of the books
are filled with big words.
Others have nothing
but pictures of birds!

Everyone was dancing 'round

with the books that they had found.

It was totally outrageous.

Reading stuff can be contagious!

Mrs. D. was really happy.

She said, "I'm so proud of Rappy."

Everybody stopped to cheer.

Now I'm Book Guy of the Year!

There were no more dirty looks
as I was checking out my books.
And even though I didn't need 'em,
I couldn't wait to sit and read 'em.

Books can teach you how to skate.

And this one helps you lose some weight.

Here's one called *The Lonely Bunny*.

This one helps you make more money.

Books on cars! Books on painting!

So many books I might be fainting!

I like sports and I like hiking.

I like swimming. I like biking.

I like cake and I like cherries.

But most of all, I like libraries!